On Mending

Stories of damage and repair

Celia Pym

Photographs by Michele Panzeri

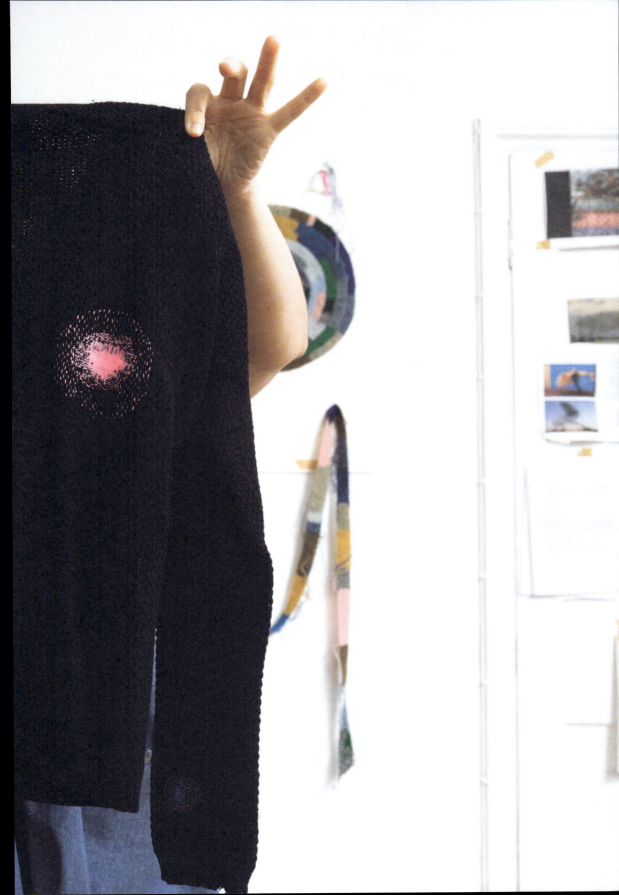

Introduction 9

Roly's Sweater 21

Elizabeth's Cardigan 27

Hope's Sweater 33

The Norwegian Sweater 39

Bill's Sweater 45

The Gold Cape 53

Lara and Lolu's Backpacks 63

Siri's Sweater 69

Vivien Leigh's Dress and Jacket 75

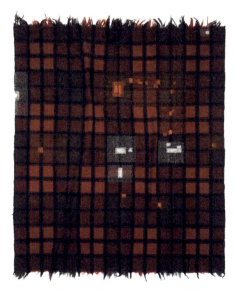
Freddie's Family Rugs 83

Celia Pym mending Paul's jumper, Radical Acts: Harewood Biennial, 2022

'Remembering the touch of someone long gone
can break your heart'

Tobin Low, 'The Ghost in the Machine', *This American Life*,
757, 31 December 2021

This book is a collection of ten stories of damaged garments – plus a rug and two backpacks – that I've mended in the last fifteen years. The stories record who the item belonged to, how it was damaged, how it was mended and where it is now.

The book is not a guide to mending techniques. It does not cover the history of mending or address questions about necessity or the need for repair. Instead, these stories describe the ways in which clothes and cloth become holed, why a damaged sweater or backpack can be emotionally affecting and how mending a garment can unstick a stuck feeling.

My interest in damaged garments began with my great-uncle Roly's sweater, which I inherited after his death and is the first story in this book. The sweater, when it came to me, had large holes in the forearms and lots of mended darns, at the elbows, cuffs and under the arms. These mends were the work of Roly's sister Elizabeth.

At that point in my life, I was not particularly interested in mending – but two things moved me about the garment. That the holes and damage were a trace of Roly's body, evocative of how he moved and wore his sweater, and that the darning marks were evidence of Elizabeth's care. These two ideas about care and the body written into worn garments have kept me curious for the past fifteen years.

Mending and the body

Mending is an action specific to cloth and the body. Textiles are mended – often the first association someone makes, if you ask them about mending, is to do with socks. They recall a grandmother, mother, aunt, uncle or father mending socks or having a mending pile. Or they recall, perhaps, a movie set in 'olden' times.

In Pedro Almodóvar's *Pain and Glory*, about a film director at the height of his career looking back at his life and recalling its tender moments, there's a touching scene where the mother, played by Penélope Cruz, spots a hole in her young son's sock, makes him take it off and mends it for him.

Celia Pym in the studio, 2022

Mending language works on the body as well as on garments. We describe the body as mending after illness or injury – 'I'm on the mend' someone might say if they're feeling better. You might hear a doctor or nurse describe a broken bone as 'mending well'. Then again broken bones are often described as knitting back together as the break heals. Textile language crops up in the body.

Garments and cloth take on a person's shape, stretched over time to the individual's form or movement. After someone has died or outgrown an item, a surviving garment is sometimes an evocative reminder of their shape and their actions. Mending can be practical and caring work for the garment and its owner.

Mending is tactile work

In 2013 I qualified as an adult nurse. Nursing teaches you to observe changes in colour, in temperature and in the pulse of a patient. These changes are sometimes described by evocative adjectives, a thready pulse, flushed cheeks, clammy skin. Observational skills seemed very important to me – small changes noticed visually or felt simply through a gentle touch.

Watching experienced nurses who could simply look at someone, or lay a hand on them for just a moment, and recognise from the subtlest change in their colour or pulse that something was wrong, was impressive. These skills felt to me like an extra sense.

I now use these observational skills when I make things or mend them, but maybe it's the other way round. Perhaps I took these skills from mending into nursing as I'd been mending for some time before I started my nursing training. I was used to noticing the thinness of cloth, an interrupted pattern in knit, the heaviness of wool, or a shift in surface and a different thread – where someone else had previously done some repair. It was a care skill felt in your hands.

Discussing holes in a blanket with the owners, Mend Event, V&A Museum, London, 2017

Mending other people's cloth and clothes can be intimate work. You put your hands where their arm or leg or foot has been. It's sensitive work, as you're holding something that's important to someone else – and damaged. Often the garment is no longer worn but not exactly ready to be discarded. One might say in these cases that it's in limbo.

Sometimes the damage in the garment is a symptom or gives a clue to some other trouble – grief or neglect, perhaps. Sometimes, however, it's wonderfully straightforward, a clean problem to be solved. But in each instance the damage leads. Mending is about responding to a problem. The repair follows where the holes are and what the material can support.

To mend a piece of clothing you must touch the cloth. Your fingers are sensitive to the texture of the fabric and fibres and your face gets close to examine the holes catching a faint smell of the owner, of perfume or washing powder, or a whiff of sweat. Mending worn cloth gets you close to another person's skin.

Looking for holes

Over the last fifteen years I have mended about five hundred garments and items belonging to all manner of different people. Occasionally, the item belonged to someone I know, a friend or a family member. More often, though, I meet the garment owner for the first time when they bring a hole and piece of clothing to be mended.

Since 2007, I've held 'Mend' events to which anyone can bring a damaged garment. The set-up includes a desk with tools and materials. Together the owner and I examine the garment and discuss the problem and the possible mending options. A variety of items have come to the mending desk. Saris with burn holes; sweaters torn on door handles; jumpers bought as a gift during an illness, now thinned by everyday use; gloves worn out from walking the dog; a cardigan with a tiny hole, that belonged to a partner who had recently died.

People bring in their own things or items that belonged to someone important to them – or perhaps were made by people they love. The mending desk asks a simple practical question. Do you have something with a hole in it or something in need of repair?

Asking people about holes in their clothes is an illuminating experience. I've found it a combination of being a textile expert, a therapist and a detective: listening to stories about garments – picking up clues about why and how the damage occurred and why it matters to the owner to mend this particular item.

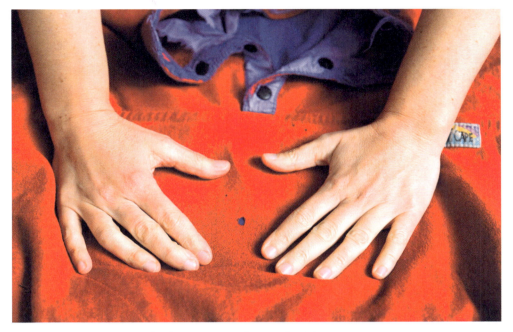

Small hole in Jim's fleece, Radical Acts: Harewood Biennial, 2022

Once I've got the holes, it often takes time to figure out the best approach to the task. Sometimes a good decision is not to mend the holes at all, simply to talk about the item was what the owner needed. And talking about a practical problem can be a good stepping-stone to revealing some buried trouble. A well-loved garment is like a second skin and can tell the story of the owner and people they've encountered and loved.

Making your fingers sensitive to damage

On a project with students studying anatomy in the dissecting room of a London teaching hospital, I came to see an overlap in the way that we use our hands and use observation to understand mending and anatomy. Students learn anatomy by studying donated bodies. It is an immense privilege to work with a donor body and one that's greatly appreciated.

Students I met described the powerful feeling of experiencing the weight or thinness of the skin of the body they were studying. The tactile sensation made an impression on them and conveyed something of the individuality of the person in front of them. While studying their donor body, the students noticed scars and evidence of past surgeries. Several commented that they found tattoos or nail polish very difficult to take, as these were more personal and immediate clues to their body's life.

Mend Event, Hockney Gallery, Royal College of Art, London, 2007

As well as learning about anatomy, how it connects and fits together in the body, the students, in this work, were developing sensitivity for the individuality of the living patients they would later encounter. Inadvertently learning that the work of care is not only about developing a broad expertise in anatomy or the pathology of an illness, but that care can also be demonstrated by looking for small clues about the story and life of the patient.

In this threshold encounter with life and death, students develop skills for noticing clues from their future patients about who they are; who they love – a tattooed name; how they like to present themselves – nail polish; a wider history of previous injury and illness – scars and stitches.

These developing skills and this sensitivity in turn helps shape decisions about approaches to care, that take into account the whole person – not only their illness. The student also learns how to navigate powerful emotional responses to what is difficult work. Feeling for damage in cloth can be helpful in making decisions on how to do the repair. You can sense, for example, whether the damage is simply from wear-and-tear. This often feels like a thinning or softening of fibres.

Moth damage, on the other hand, has a distinctively different feel. Sometimes the moths haven't eaten all the way through the fabric, but by running your fingers over the cloth you can identify by the uneven surface where they've nibbled. And if the garment hasn't been washed, there'll be the grainy feel of dead eggs.

With more dramatic damage, such as fire, the fibres might be 'sticky' or crispy at the edge of the damage. Whereas a tear or scrape caused by an accident often feels sharp. And on soft fabric, the edge is often cleaner. It's as if, in a sense, the threads have been 'shocked'.

Once I encountered a garment damaged by fire and I was struck by the thought that the person must have been quite distracted not to notice that their top was on fire. The owner of the garment was in fact deep in grief for his wife who had died not long before. We talked about the top and its large burnt hole, but mainly we talked about his wife.

Looking at The Gold Cape with students from Blönduós, Iceland, 2016

Making visible what's missing

Mending is always in response to a problem. The damage leads and the mending follows. With darning and patching – mending techniques I use most often – the choices and decisions about how wide to reinforce, what materials to use, or which direction to take the mending, is led by the nature and quality of the damage.

Decisions are also informed by what the owner wants from their mended item. If they wish to wear it again, the mend needs to be robust, if they wish to pack it away and conserve it the mend can be gentler.

I like to mend so that you can see what's missing and what has been lost. To mend with a contrasting colour to highlight the hole is a distinctly confident move. It makes visible the change in the garment, its aging and its life. It makes the thing different and new with a fresh colour. And then when mended again, in the future, with another colour, this will add an additional layer to the story of the garment.

Mending work builds on what is left behind. It's not replacing, or remaking, or cutting apart and putting back together, instead it is slow work that makes things better. It conjures an unhurried recovery or change. In textiles, the act of mending wear-and-tear, thinning cloth or accidental damage builds on what already exists, anchoring threads and yarn into the robust healthy fabric and filling in the holes or reinforcing the areas that are weak.

This is true in the body too. It takes time for broken bones to knit together and for wounds to heal by bridging the gap of an injury. Mending layers on top of what was already there, stitching the damage into the story of the cloth, and like a scar on the human body it tells a story worthy of our attention.

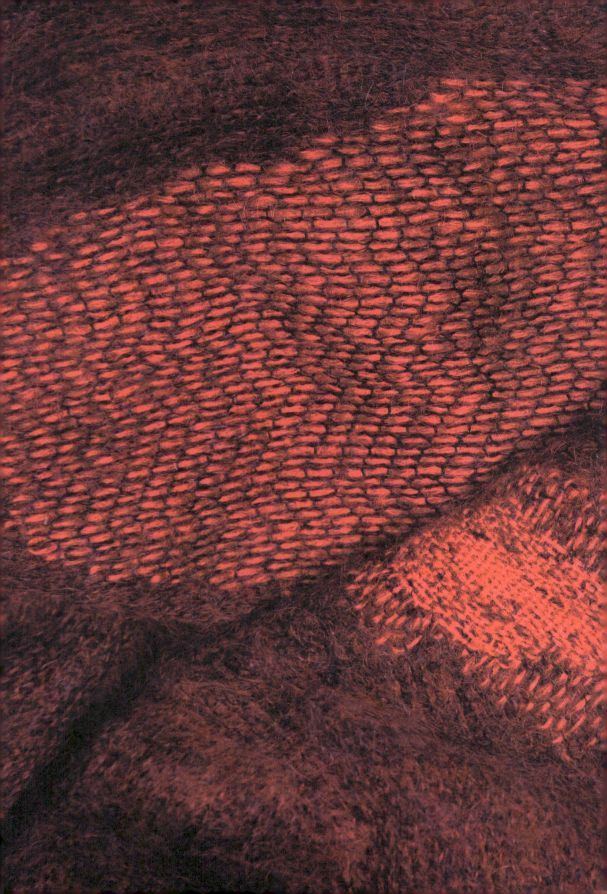

Stories

Roly's Sweater

Eighty years old, mended 2007

Roland Pym's sweater was hand-knitted – probably by his sister Elizabeth, in or around 1940. Family lore has it that Elizabeth, my great-aunt, knitted the sweater for her husband Patrick Cobb whom she married in 1941. After Patrick, a Lieutenant in the Royal Naval Volunteer Reserve, was killed in action in the English Channel in 1942, the sweater was given as a remembrance to his brother-in-law Roland.

Roly in his armchair, 1999

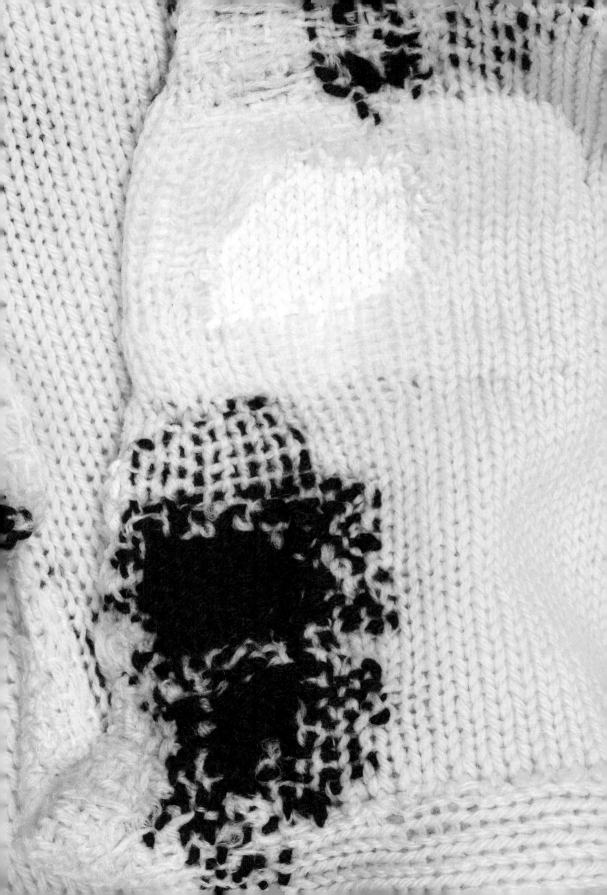

Roly worked as a painter, muralist and book illustrator. He drew or painted, it seems, every day of his life since childhood. He never married and died in his ninety-sixth year.

The sweater had lots of holes from wear-and-tear. Elizabeth, with whom Roly lived after the Second World War, mended the sweater many times. She used white and cream yarn. They are robust and ready darns, sometimes thin repairs in a variety of mismatched wools and cotton. There's a knitted square used to patch a hole inside the elbow and some yarn is threaded through the thinning cuffs. The darning feels direct and has a practical quality that reminded me of Elizabeth herself – unfussy and not particularly decorative, but still full of care.

Towards the end of his life, Roly would spend most days seated in his armchair drawing – his forearms rested on a drawing board, wearing down the sleeves as he leant forward and worked. Elizabeth died four years before Roly and these new forearm holes in the sweater emerged in the years after her death. Looking for guidance in Elizabeth's stitches, I mended the forearm holes in blue with plain, woven darns. The holes were repaired in blue so that the stitches would be a different colour to Elizabeth's. When the darning was done the blue made the pattern of wear and damage visible. The contrast revealed what was missing.

Roly's Sweater is kept in a box and occasionally sent around the world to exhibitions. Even in its box, however, the sweater continues to age – and to develop holes. These are not moth holes, just a sort of thinning of yarn. Before each new exhibition, there's usually a little mending to be done.

Elizabeth's Cardigan

Fifty to seventy years old, mended 2007 to 2020

Elizabeth was married to Patrick Cobb who died in the Second World War. She kept three small black-and-white photographs of her husband beside her bed for the rest of her life. In one, Patrick, a tall serious man, sits on a lawn in his shirtsleeves with an arm circling a little shaggy poodle.

Roly Pym and Elizabeth Cobb, 2000

During the war Elizabeth worked for the Red Cross in Kent. She had no children of her own, but for many years after the war helped to organise camping holidays for children with disabilities, and she particularly enjoyed teaching riding to children from a local school for the blind.

In the 1980s and 90s, Elizabeth, with whom my parents and my brother and sister and I then lived, wore sensible shoes with flesh-coloured tights, knee-length skirts and lightweight floral blouses. She kept her grey hair short. She was a dedicated gardener and vegetable grower, and she often appears, in my memory, with an old trug over her arm containing gloves and secateurs.

Patrick Cobb, 1941

Elizabeth always had a dog, a black Standard poodle. When one died, she bought another. In cool weather she wore a collared puffy green jacket or duffel coat. She was practical and efficient in everything she did. She knew how to make a cake without a recipe and how to fix a leaking roof.

There are two patch pockets at the front of Elizabeth's Cardigan. She kept tissues and hankies in her pockets, and Fox's Glacier Mints – a clear shiny hardboiled sweet – for afternoon walks. It's not known when or how Elizabeth acquired the cardigan. It was made by Murray Brothers woollen mill in Hawick, a town in the Scottish Borders.

Perhaps she bought it on holiday in Scotland, or perhaps it was a Christmas present from her much-loved father.

The elbows became threadbare from repeated wear. The knitting was so thin it looked like a fine spider's web. The elbows are reinforced with navy wool. The reinforcing didn't last long, new holes appeared at the edge of the reinforced areas. The new holes were mended with a bright blue. The darning has gone wide to strengthen the fragile thin areas and then is woven at the hole. The cuffs and hems were frayed and reinforced and there were a few moth holes darned with a variety of white wools. I sometimes take Elizabeth's Cardigan from its storage box and hang it on the back on my studio chair.

Elizabeth Cobb with Celia, 1980

Hope's Sweater

Seventy years old, mended 2009

Hope Auerbach, my Mum, was about three years old in the photo on the next page. She's wearing a Fair Isle sweater and matching beret bought by her mother, Judy, on a trip to London in 1951. At the time, Hope was living with her parents and her older brother, Jonny, in Düsseldorf on the Rhine. Her father, Joe, a lawyer, was working for the United States Government on the decartelisation of the German steel industry. It was Joe who took this first photograph of Hope's Sweater. A label identifies it as having being hand-knitted in Shetland.

Judy's family – Grammy's family – owned the Evans Department Store in Berlin, New Hampshire. The store sold everything. Grammy, however, was not cut out for business – nor did she have an especially practical nature. She was more interested in style. She loved and looked great in neat, waisted dresses, patterned and chequered fabrics, and she always had gloves and scarves that matched her look.

She was a university librarian and paid attention to how she dressed for work. In pictures of her in the 1950s and 60s, she comes across as very glamorous. I have a photo of her – pinned to the back of my kitchen door – looking relaxed in sunglasses, shorts and a top that tied at the front, sitting in a fold-up chair on the beach, her legs stretched and feet digging into the sand. It makes sense to me that she would have bought her daughter this beautiful sweater – and on the same trip to London a stylish scarf and cardigan for herself.

In the early 1980s, Hope's Sweater became part of my brother William's wardrobe. He outgrew it and our mother packed it away for twenty-five years. When it was rediscovered, in 2008, the moths had done their work. A whole section at the front below the collar had almost turned to dust. Holding this sweater now, I can clearly remember struggling as a child to lift up my little brother. Today the scale of the child's sweater makes a powerful impact on me. It's hard, somehow, to reconcile the size of a grown-up person – both William and my mother – with the smallness of the garment they used to fit into.

For the mend, I picked out a heathery purple colour from the pattern. The small holes are darned and the large section of damage at the front was filled in with a knitted patch. There was a tiny red fragment of knitting in the middle of the large eaten-away section. Trying to hold on to that piece was a delicate business. The cuffs needed a lot of attention. They've been darned a little too tight, making them lose some of their stretchiness.

The sweater is wrapped in tissue paper in a box and has travelled the world for exhibitions – most recently going to Switzerland for the show 'Material Matters' at the Textile Museum in St Gallen.

Judy Auerbach, Düsseldorf, 1951

Hope Auerbach wearing her sweater and beret, 1951

Celia with Hope, 1979

William in his mother's sweater, 1985

The Norwegian Sweater

Fifty to eighty years old, mended 2009

This sweater comes from Annemor Sundbø's collection, 'Treasures from a Ragpile', in Setesdal, Norway. Annemor ran a shoddy factory, Torridal Tweed, from 1983 to 2006. Its purpose was recycling used clothing. While feeding her shredding machine, often with hand-knitted knitwear, she started to notice items that she felt shouldn't go through the shoddy machine. She would save these garments and slowly amassed a one-tonne collection of second-hand knitwear. Much of the knitwear has evidence of or clues to the lives of the owners – lots of careful re-use and salvaging of materials and mending due to need and necessity.

The Norwegian Sweater before mending

Annemor Sundbø sorting through her Ragpile, 1980s

There was extensive damage and many holes in The Norwegian Sweater when Annemor first gave it to me. The sweater is narrow waisted with broad shoulders. Both arms were ruined, the wool was felted and matted in places and one sleeve was dangling by a thread. The back had a huge hole and both the back and front hems were worn down. The front of the sweater has a deep 'v' and was missing fastenings that would have held it together – rust marks in the wool along the edge of the 'v' indicating the missing fastenings.

Annemor Sundbø in front of Torridal Tweed, Setesdal, 1980s

There is no label and the garment looks and feels like a hand-knitted sweater. On one sleeve the dark navy yarn was replaced with a purple at some point – the original knitter had perhaps run out of black, or later maybe, the sleeve had been damaged. The cuffs had been mended by many hands. The fresh damage is mended in white – picking out the white already in the pattern. The missing parts were so large that the white darns started to look like snow blown across the sweater.

    This sweater is kept in a flat box. It lies neatly inside a foam cut-out of itself. It comes out for exhibitions and in the last ten years has travelled to Norway, Japan, America, Spain and France.

Snapshot of sweater in Annemor Sundbø's collection in Ose near Setesdal, 2009

Washing line in Annemor's collection, Ose, 2009

Annemor's shop and Ragpile Museum, Ose, 2009

Bill's Sweater

Twenty to thirty years old, mended 2010 to 2017

'One of the things that disappeared with Bill was the jumper,' Sarah Bold, Bill's daughter, wrote to me in an email on 14 May 2021. Bill Smith was a family doctor in Muswell Hill, North London. He was also a Slade-trained painter and sculptor. His wife Ursie was a painter and every wall of their house was covered with her watercolours and drawings, and his oil paintings and sketches.

Bill Smith and Celia, Muswell Hill, 2017

Bill and Ursie's home had a slightly wild and – at the same time – soft tone. Books and papers seemed to be piled everywhere, and both the walls and the furnishings were in distinctively cool muted colours. Ursie liked to wear loose pale-pastel lightweight dresses with sandals – and she made delicious almond macaroons.

Bill Smith at his kitchen table, 2017

The colours Bill loved to wear included pinks and purples, yellows and oranges. He embraced bright colour. When I went to discuss mending an item for Bill – this was after Ursie's death – we found a drawer at the bottom of his bedroom cupboard with four or five hand-knitted sweaters. All had been quite badly damaged by moths.

We took out an orange one and looked at it together. This led to talk about Ursie who'd hand-knitted the sweater. Bill told me how once, in Greece, Ursie had seen a very complicated hat that took her fancy. She examined it and when they got home knitted it from memory. Bill had chosen the sweater's orange colour – Ursie preferred more muted tones – and Ursie knitted it up without measuring him. According to Bill, she knew the shape of him in her fingers.

Bill's Sweater was damaged particularly at the front where it had been folded. Bill's daughter, Martha Knox Forrester, had mended the sweater, as had Nathalie Viera, the girlfriend of one of Bill's grandsons. The fresh moth damage was repaired with bright yellow wool.

The sweater and a portrait of Bill wearing it were exhibited around the UK, including at the V&A Museum, London. Bill and his neighbour Alan Morton came to the opening at the V&A where Bill was the star of the show. People wanted to shake his hand – they'd seen his portrait on the wall. They even wanted to take pictures with him standing in front of his sweater.

Ursie Smith in Mallorca, 1998

Bill died in 2020 after a short stay in a care home. His daughter Sarah says she's not sure where the orange sweater is now. She asked her sister Martha and they wondered if perhaps it was simply mislaid at the care home. Bill was only at the home for ten days before going to hospital where, shortly afterwards, he died. Sarah said maybe there is someone at the care home wearing the sweater. I hope so. It was a home that specialised in dementia care.

Bill in his garden studio, Muswell Hill, 2017

The Gold Cape

Eighty to one hundred years old, mended 2016 to 2018

The Gold Cape comes from the archive collection of the Nouveau Musée National de Monaco (NMNM). Its precise history is unknown, but what is known is that it belonged originally to the Monte Carlo Opera House costume collection and was later donated to the NMNM archive.

Ate wearing The Gold Cape, Blönduós, 2018

Danny wrapped in The Gold Cape, London, 2018

The cape is wide, longer than the span of a pair of arms, and sequins radiate down the back, increasing in size from the neck to the hem. There are two fabric handles, positioned so that when you grip them your hands rest on your breastbone. If you stretch your arms out wide and hold the edge, the cape hangs off your arms like wings.

The cape was in an in-between state for many years – too damaged for display, but even in its damaged state retaining the energy and potential to inspire an audience.

When I first saw the cape, with Célia Bernasconi, the museum curator, and Anne-Sophie Loussouarn, the costume caretaker, it was stored in a plastic bag. The handles were draped over a hanger and the bulk of the cape rested at the bottom of the bag. The silk layer with the sequins had come away from the top edge and was tangled up. The silk was very fragile and would crumble in your fingers when handled. The cape was one of fifty-nine items labelled 'S'. This stood for 'sortie' – meaning it was getting ready to exit the collection because its provenance was unknown and its damage so extensive it was difficult to know what to do with it.

When we spread The Gold Cape on a table it was possible to pull apart and piece together the fragments. Threaded sequins worked as a delicate spider's-web structure to guide us. It took five months to mend the silk layer and restore it to a wearable condition. The fragments of silk and loose sequins were stitched in place on the cotton backing-cloth with silk and metallic thread. The corners, where there was most damage, were patched to cover the holes. Thousands of stitches were required to hold it all together. This made the cape heavier than it was originally. The additional thread worked to quilt the layers together. The new weight did not, however, impede the elegance or grace of the cape's movement.

Once mended, I took The Gold Cape out in the world to be worn and performed in. First stop Blönduós, northwest Iceland – to visit a residential home, primary school and colleagues at Textilseturs, an art textile centre. I had been resident at the centre while mending the cape and some of the children in the town had worn it mid-mend. Jóhanna Erla Pálmadóttir, a farmer and director of the foundation, took us to a view overlooking her farm. She kicked off her shoes and stood barefoot and rooted, the wind whipping around her, and posed in profile.

Then on to France, where a woman draped the cape over her shoulders – and launched with gusto into an Edith Piaf song. In Monaco, we returned the cape to the Monte Carlo Opera House where it was

Jóhanna Erla Pálmadóttir, Blönduós, 2018

originally worn and gave it to children and a theatre group to pose in around the auditorium, backstage and on stage. In London, we visited a primary school where children made drawings of the cape and then paraded around the school standing ready for their portraits. In the playground they ran about with the cape flying behind them.

Over the course of the tour, The Gold Cape became more damaged, sequins fell off, more of the silk disintegrated. The beauty of the cape was the way it transformed people when they wore it. Wearers would stand straighter or have an impulse to run, spin and wrap it around their bodies. The wearers struck poses and attitudes inspired by how they felt in the cape. After touring and much mending – not quite as shiny as when it was first made – The Gold Cape acquired a new set of stories. Being worn, it came alive

The Gold Cape belongs to the NMNM archive. It is handled with care. When it was displayed in 2018, it took at least four people to lift and hang it, coordinating movements and delicately placing it on the wall – quite different from being thrown over shoulders on windy hills or being twirled by small children who disappeared inside it.

NMNM team hanging the cape, 2018

A theatre group performer, Monte Carlo Opera House, 2018

Cap Fleuri carer and resident, France, 2018

The Mending Desk in the Dissecting Room, KCL, 2014

Lara and Lolu's Backpacks

Ten to eleven years old, mended 2014

Lara Veitch and Lolu Oluwole-Ojo, seen on the following pages with their backpacks, were anatomy students. They participated in a project called 'Mending and Anatomy: Parallel Practices', which placed mending clothes next to the study of human anatomy in the heart of the Dissecting Room at King's College London.

The Dissecting Room (DR) at KCL is a space, licensed under the Human Tissue Act (2004) and regulated by the Human Tissue Authority, where students study anatomy on human cadavers. For this project, in partnership with Dr Richard Wingate, students were invited to bring damaged items of their own in for repair. The idea was to offer them – and their damaged items – care and attention. And at the same time to see if there was something more about care and materials the students could learn in the DR beyond anatomy.

Lolu's Backpack had torn at the shoulder strap, but he'd continued to carry it about on the other strap, though that one was also starting to show signs of strain. The fabric on Lara's Backpack had become thin and torn at the top edge by the zip – caused by pressure closing the bag when it was too full. Lolu's bag was a practical bag that he'd bought for school. He liked it because it was fit for purpose, reliable and didn't attract attention. He was disappointed the strap had come loose – because, as he said, it was a good bag that did the job. Lara's connection to her bag was different. She'd had her bag since childhood in Kenya and was attached to it for sentimental reasons. It had crossed continents with her.

Lara with her backpack, 2014

Lolu with his backpack, 2014

Both bags had become damaged from carrying heavy books. Lolu was keen to have his bag mended discreetly – to return it to the look it had when it was new. Lara was excited about having a visible patch to highlight the life of the bag. Both backpacks were repaired and returned to their owners – after which I lost touch with Lara and Lolu.

Lara Veitch in her uncle's plane with her tattoos

Several years later, in the course of research for this book, I learned that Lara had left King's suffering from cancer and that she went on to work for charities and as a spokesperson for young adults with cancer at the National Cancer Research Institute.

Lara met Bryony Kimmings, the artist who wrote the musical *A Pacifist's Guide to the War on Cancer*. They became friends and went on to perform together in a production of the musical produced by the Complicité theatre company that toured England and Australia. In a video for this project, Lara speaks movingly about her experiences.

She died in 2020. I wrote to Lara's father, Justin, asking permission to share his daughter's image and story. 'Unfortunately,' he replied, 'we don't know where her backpack is now, possibly her best friend who lived with her has it, but we remember it well. Lara got it as a child, possibly when we lived in Kenya, and used it for many years. She was very attached to it. Lara believed in embracing repair and you may be interested to know that when she had a double mastectomy, instead of hiding it or getting an implant she had a glorious and colourful tattoo across her chest which she was very proud of.'

Lara and Lolu with their classmates and KCL staff, 2014

Siri's Sweater

Four years old, mended 2020

Siri Johansen is a knitwear designer and founder of the company WYP – Waste Yarn Project, Paris. This sweater was made by L.L.Bean, an American outdoor wear company. Their tag line is the 'Outside Is Inside Everything We Make'. Siri has no sentimental attachment to the sweater, it came from a market or a second-hand shop – she can't remember exactly.

Testing yarns and preparing to mend Siri's Sweater, 2019

Growing up in Norway, Siri says, 'You learn to knit in school. My Mum and Grandmas were great hand-knitters, they taught me most of what I know today. Importantly, I learnt from them how to freestyle and make up my own patterns. But it was not until I started studying in the UK that I became more interested in knitting as a material and looked back to my Norwegian knitting heritage with fresh eyes.'

A few years back, Siri had an idea that required only half a sweater. She says that in the studio they often cut garments up and play around with them. So she cut her sweater in half.

Siri's Sweater cut in half, 2019

Sometime later, packing a box and clearing up, she found two halves of the sweater and passed them to me – thinking I might do something with them. There was cleanness to the cut of this damage and as a result a clarity and straightness to the mend – the blue darn looks like a scar. The scissors were quick to cut the sweater in half and the needle was slow darning it back together – opposite but complementary actions and tools. Siri's Sweater was returned to her in Paris. Her young son, she reports, sometimes wraps himself up in it.

Mending in progress

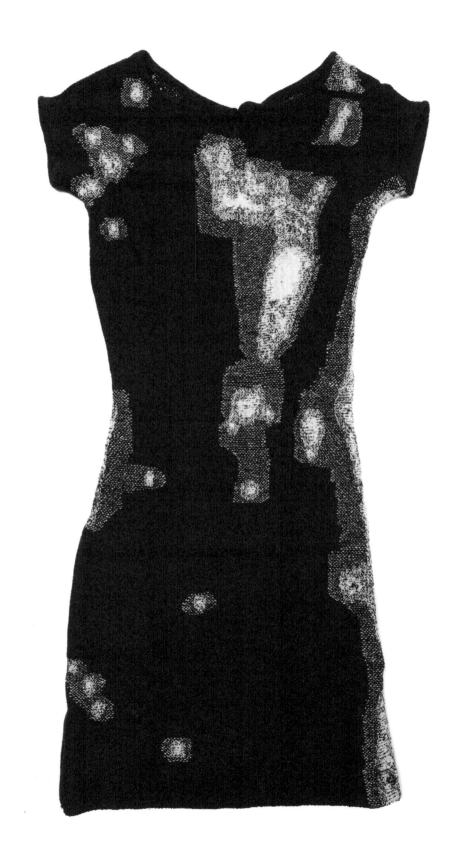

Vivien Leigh's Dress and Jacket

Fifty-six years old, mended 2020

This dress and jacket ensemble belonged to the British actress Vivien Leigh, one of the great stars of her day, celebrated for such films as *Gone With the Wind* and *A Streetcar Named Desire*. The garments lay forgotten in an attic for fifty-odd years before being rediscovered in 2018. But by then the dress and jacket had been devoured by moths.

Vivien Leigh and her husband Laurence Olivier, 1956

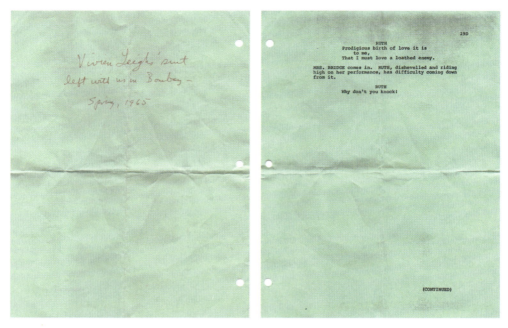

Note from James Ivory that came with the garments written on the back of page from a script, 2019

The American film director James Ivory, who passed the ensemble to me, writes that he and his partner, the producer Ismail Merchant, met Vivien Leigh in Bombay, now Mumbai, in 1965. They were making their second feature film, *Shakespeare Wallah*, and she was passing through on her way to Darjeeling, West Bengal, where she'd spent her childhood.

Vivien, it seems, packed poorly or too hastily. These wool garments were unsuited to the Indian climate. Ismail, however, with his customary lack of hesitation, instantly offered to look after the garments, along with some other items, so Vivien could travel more easily. He would return everything to her at a later date when they could meet in New York or London.

But the reunion to retrieve the clothes never happened, and Vivien Leigh died two years after the meeting in Bombay. In due course, Vivien Leigh's Dress and Jacket found its way to Jim's house at Claverack in upstate New York. 'It looked like road kill!' Jim said when, many years later, he finally re-opened the box in which the clothes were stored.

The ensemble is a wool-and-silk hand-knitted cloth, made by the Women's Home Industries (WHI), a company founded in London in 1947. The aim of the WHI was to harness women's craft skills in order to

Vivien Leigh's Dress before mending, 2019

develop economic independence. Women could work from home sending pieces of knitting in to headquarters to be stitched up into garments.

In the WHI archive, held at London College of Fashion, UAL, there are newspaper clippings about the business and its success. Response to a call out for 'would be knitters' was overwhelming – 31,000 people applied. Through clever marketing and excellent product, WHI knitwear became desirable with actresses and society women.

The archive includes client guest books. Eleanor Roosevelt's signature appears twice in 1959. There are samples in the archive similar to Vivien Leigh's Dress and Jacket that suggest it was a ready-to-wear item, trendy and desirable. It's not known if Vivien Leigh bought the outfit especially for the trip to India or had owned it for some time. Although it's extensively damaged, it doesn't look very well worn.

Press cuttings, WHI Archive

There was a great deal of moth dust on the garments when they arrived back in England from New York – a combination of old eggs, moth wings, wispy half-eaten remnants of wool. The garments needed careful washing to see the extent of the damage. But even then fragments of wool fell away. The bigger fragments were saved and stitched back in place.

The main fabric is knitted in a moss stitch. It's fine and lightweight. The jacket has a lilac and black mohair trim that looks a bit like fake fur. The dress has a surprisingly large 40cm hem. As if, when it was fitted, it was too long and had been hemmed in a hurry.

It's such a fine knit wool that, handling it today, I find that the knitters and their fingers come to mind. I'm impressed by the delicacy of the work and also curious about how the knitters felt about their work. Did they see famous actresses in the press wearing garments they'd hand-knitted? The archive indicates a fashion-forward company, modern and fun.

The moth holes are mended with warm, white cashmere wool from Japan. The white was chosen to be a strong contrast to the dark purple – and a luxury fibre to match the quality outfit. The idea was – through the white mending – to hold the damage in place and at the same time to evoke something of Jim Ivory's reaction when he rediscovered Vivien Leigh's Dress and Jacket in his attic – not exactly 'road kill', but a damaged and dusty two-piece, caught up in ancient cobwebs.

Well-used pattern book, WHI Archive

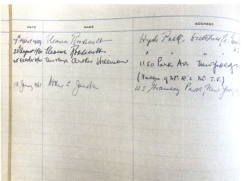

Guest book with Eleanor Roosevelt's signature, WHI Archive

Freddie's Family Rugs

Sixty years old, mended 2022

These red rugs belonged to Freddie Robins' family. They were used for picnics and outdoor events. You can see them in use in the photographs on the following pages. Freddie is an artist, Senior Tutor and Reader in Textiles at the Royal College of Art, London.

Molly Robins, her sister Peggy and brother-in-law Pip

Freddie, Molly and Sallie Robins, Dordogne, France, 1983

Sallie and Ronald Robins, France, 1980

Molly, Pip and Peggy

Peggy, Molly and Pip, Brittany, France, 1980

Freddie and her nephew Robbie, 2000

Sallie and Willa Coode-Robins, 2004

Willa, 2004

Freddie's parents were Ronald (Frederick George) Robins and mum Molly (Chisholm) Woolley, becoming Molly (Chisholm) Robins. Freddie says, 'My Mum was seven years older than my Dad. My Dad was a practical, well-prepared person and loved motoring, so he always had at least one rug in the boot of the car, should it be needed for a picnic in the summer or to keep warm if the car broke down in winter.

'The car was spotless. It had to be. It was a company car and keeping your car spotless was one of the terms of agreement for having a company car. I wish that I knew where the rugs came from. They may have been a wedding present. My parents married in 1963. If they were wedding presents, then the rugs are nearly sixty years old. I don't remember them ever being new.' Of the family rugs, Freddie says, 'They always felt so contemporary, compared with the traditional wool blanket. My Mum loved modern things. Probably a reaction to being a teenager during the war.' Of the snapshots, 'My dad must have been taking the photographs. He was a terrible photographer, but a great father.'

After her parents died, Freddie went through their house and found the rugs and these photographs. One rug had holes in it. The damage was a combination of moth holes, a burn and general wear-and-tear at the edges. It's hard work going through possessions after someone you love has died. The items are so familiar and evocative of your past, but at the same time don't always fit in the present. Freddie didn't want to discard one particular rug, but was uncertain exactly what to do with it.

Discussing what colours to mend in, Freddie picked out the orange plastic cool box as a reference. She wrote 'Being the 1970s we had a lot of orange plastic stuff. Maybe 1970s plastic picnic-ware is the way to go, synthetic colours.'

This rug is thickly woven wool and the moths have struggled to eat all the way through. Their damage is more like a thinning. When you hold it up to the light, in places you can almost see through it. The burn is a distinctive square hole. Burns often have clear defined edges – suggesting that something really is missing, a proper absence. My intention was to make the mend 'modern'. Using a combination of orange and white. The mend is intended to be bold and in no way discreet. This should, I hope, become a real picnic rug again in the future.

'When I look at all these photographs I realise that the blankets were ever present,' Freddie said. 'They were silent, useful members of the family.'

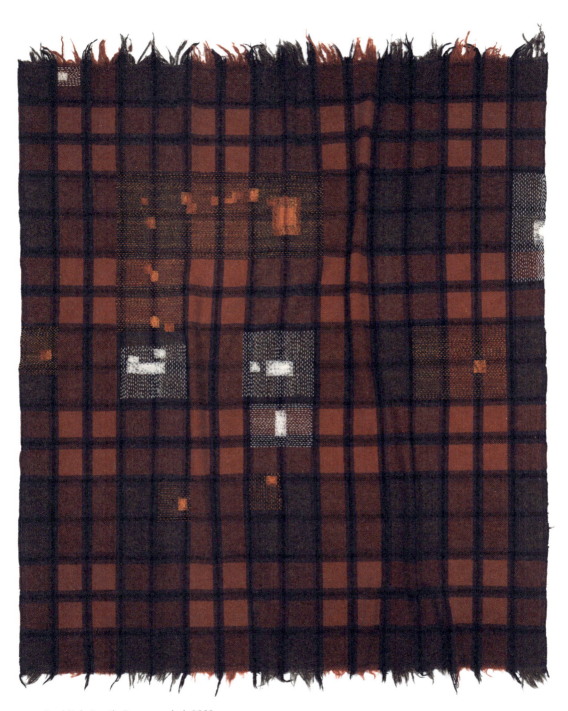

Freddie's Family Rug, mended, 2022

Biography

Celia Pym lives in London and has been exploring damage and repair in textiles since 2007. Working with garments that belong to individuals as well as items in museum archives, she has broad experience with stories of damage, from moth holes to accidents with fire. She's interested in exploring the varied evidence of damage, and how repair draws attention to the places where garments and cloth wear down and grow thin. 'Darning is small acts of care,' she says, 'and paying close attention.'

Her work has been exhibited most recently in 'Keep Being Amazing', Firstsite, Colchester, Essex (2022), 'Waste Age', Design Museum, London (2021), and 'On Happiness: Joy + Tranquillity', Wellcome Collection, London (2021). She is an Associate Lecturer in Textiles at the Royal College of Art in London.

Acknowledgements

Celia Pym would like to thank the following individuals for their help in the development of this book: Karin Andreasson, Julie Arkell, Célia Bernasconi, Katy Bevan, Sarah Bold, Bill Bragg, El Brown, James Ivory, Siri Johansen, Rachael Matthews, Fraser Muggeridge, Lina Peterson, the Pym family, Freddie Robins, Annemor Sundbø, Justin Veitch, Manon Veyssière and Richard Wingate.

Picture credits

I am grateful to Michele Panzeri who has been photographing my work with an immensely sympathetic eye since 2010. All the photographs in this book are Michele's unless otherwise specified:

Celia Pym, 14, 21, 42–43, 53, 58, 69–71, 78–79
Cornelia Theimer Gardella, 15
Hope and John Pym, 28–29, 34–35
Annemor Sundbø, 40–41
Sarah Bold, 47
Justin Veitch, 66
Getty Images, 75
Freddie Robins, 83–85

Contents:

Hope's Sweater, 1951
Celia Pym

Child's sweater and framed photographs

On Mending © 2022 Celia Pym

Celia Pym is hereby identified as the author of this work in accordance with section 77 of the Copyright, Designs and Patent Act, 1988. She asserts and gives notice of her moral right under this Act.

Published by Quickthorn
Elm Cottage, Dark Lane, Chalford GL6 8QD, England
info@quickthornbooks.com
www.quickthornbooks.com

All rights reserved. No part of this book may be reproduced, stored in a retrieval system or transmitted in any form by any means (electronic or mechanical, through reprography, digital transmission, recording or otherwise) without prior written permission of the publisher.

Editor: Katy Bevan
Design and typesetting by Fraser Muggeridge studio

Printed in the UK by Cambrian Printers
Printed on environmentally friendly chlorine-free paper sourced from renewable forest stock

British Library Cataloguing in Publication Data applied for
ISBN 978-1-912480-58-6